D0772581

The Checkered Flag

Formula 1 Racing

Paul Challen

PowerKiDS
press

New York

Published in 2015 by **The Rosen Publishing Group, Inc.**
29 East 21st Street, New York, NY 10010

Library of Congress Cataloging-in-Publication-Data
Challen, Paul.
Formula 1 racing / by Paul Challen.
p. cm. — (The checkered flag)
Includes index.
ISBN 978-1-4994-0169-1 (pbk.)
ISBN 978-1-4994-0138-7 (6-pack)
ISBN 978-1-4994-0161-5 (library binding)
1. Grand Prix racing — Juvenile literature. 2. Formula One automobiles — Juvenile literature.
3. Automobile racing — Juvenile literature. I. Challen, Paul C. (Paul Clarence), 1967-. II. Title.
GV1029.C425 2015
796.72 —d23

Developed and produced for Rosen by BlueAppleWorks Inc.
Art Director: Tibor Choleva
Managing Editor for BlueAppleWorks: Melissa McClellan
Designer: Joshua Avramson
Photo Research: Jane Reid
Editor: Marcia Abramson

Photo Credits: Cover ©David Acosta Allely/Shutterstock; Title page ©Alexander Sandvoss/Dreamstime; TOC ©Grand
Prix/Keystone Press; p. 4–5 ©Euriico/Dreamstime; p.5 top ©Nikolai Sorokin/Dreamstime; p. 5 bottom Phanuruch8555/
Creative Commons; p. 6–7 Library of Congress/Public Domain; p. 6 top ©Rui Ferreira/Shutterstock; p. 7 bottom Edwin
van Nes/Creative Commons; p. 7 right ©Sergey Goryache/Shutterstock; p. 8 Morio/Creative Commons; p. 9 left
©Digitalsport/Dreamstime; p. 9 right, p. 16–17 ©Jeff Schultes/Shutterstock; p. 10–11 ©Natursports/Shutterstock; p. 10
top ©David Acosta Allely/Shutterstock; p. 11 right, 12 bottom ©MrSegui/Shutterstock; p. 12 top Ryan Bayona/Creative
Commons; p. 13 bottom, 14 top ©ZRyzner/Shutterstock; p. 13 right ©Jon Buckle/Keystone Press; p. 14-15 bottom
©Jarnogz /Dreamstime; p. 15 left ©Patrik Dietrich/Shutterstock; p. 15 top ©Digitalsport/Dreamstime; p. 16 top ©Serjio74/
Shutterstock; p. 17 right ©Manwolste/Dreamstime; p. 18–19 bottom ©Eniko Balogh/Shutterstock; p. 18 top ©Eniko
Balogh/Dreamstime; p. 19 right ©Mypokcik/Dreamstime; p. 20 top, bottom ©Chen Ws /Shutterstock; p. 22–23, 23 right
©Fifian Iromi/Shutterstock; p. 24 left ©Dana Gardner/Shutterstock; p. 24 top ©Mikhail Kolesnikov /Shutterstock; p. 25, 26
bottom ©Imago/Keystone Press; p. 25 right ©Dr Ajay Kumar Singh /Dreamstime; p. 26 top ©Shaiful Rizal Mohd Jaafar/
Dreamstime; p. 27 left ©Pyshnyy Maxim Vjacheslavovich/Shutterstock; p. 27 right senna.org.br/Creative Commons; p. 27
bottom ©David Acosta Allely/Shutterstock; p. 28 top ©Jordan Tan/Shutterstock; p. 28–29 ©Neacsu Razvan Chirnoaga/
Dreamstime; p. 28 right ©Glenda Powers/Dreamstime; p. 28 left ©Wangkun Jia/Dreamstime; p. 29 top ©TachePhoto/
Shutterstock

Manufactured in the United States of America

CPSIA Compliance Information: Batch #CW15PK: For Further Information contact: Rosen Publishing, New York, New York at 1-800-237-9932

Table of Contents

What Is Formula 1?

Formula 1 is a type of car racing. The cars that compete in Formula 1 follow a set of rules, or formula, about how the cars can be constructed and how races are run.

Formula 1 racing, also called F1, is extremely popular all over the world. The sport's annual championship is made up of a series of up to 20 races, in locations in North and South America, Europe, Asia, and Australia. Individual races are known as **Grand Prix** races, and are usually named after the places that hold them. Examples are the British, Malaysian, and Canadian Grand Prix.

The cars that race in Formula 1 are the most advanced of all the formula race cars.

Global Popularity

Because of this global reach, Formula 1 is one of the top five spectator sports in the world. Grand Prix races draw more than 120,000 spectators to the course. Over the three days of a Formula 1 race, more than 300,000 people can attend an event. It is estimated that about 30 million people in 150 countries watch each race on television.

An organization called **FIA** (Fédération Internationale de l'Automobile, which is French for International Automobile Federation) controls Formula 1 racing. FIA got its start in 1904, back in the early days of motor cars. The association has grown to include 236 national racing organizations in 141 countries. FIA determines the sport's rules and the annual world championship.

The Formula 1 World Championship season consists of a series of races, known as Grand Prix, usually held on tracks built just for racing.

The FIA headquarters are in Paris, France.

The History of Formula 1

When cars first started racing, there were no limits on how big or powerful they could be. This was dangerous, so early race organizers made rules about the size and power of racing cars. These rules were called a formula.

Organizers got the idea for Formula 1 from Grand Prix races held in Europe during the 1920s and 1930s. World War II slowed down the planning, but the first Formula 1 races were held in 1946 just after the war ended. By 1947 race organizers already were planning to start a drivers' championship.

Early models of Formula 1 cars still race in exhibition car events.

In the early part of the twentieth century, races between high-performance cars were very popular.

Off to a Fast Start

⚠ **FAST FACT**

The name Formula 1 was chosen to indicate the top, or No. 1, form of auto racing.

By spring 1950, all the rules for Formula 1 were ready, and the first F1 championship was held in Silverstone, England.

An Alfa Romeo driver, Giuseppe Farina of Italy, won the first championship. The most famous driver of the 1950s, though, was Juan Manuel Fangio of Argentina, who won in 1951, 1954, 1955, 1956, and 1957. He drove for all the top F1 automakers of that era: Alfa Romeo, Ferrari, Maserati, and Mercedes Benz.

Formula 1 was on its way. In the next decades, races became better organized and fans flocked to the sport.

Many countries issued postal stamps to honor Juan Manuel Fangio, an early Formula 1 star. This stamp is from Guinea.

This historical collection of Ferrari Formula 1 cars shows the progress of car designs.

The Formula

The formula that these cars follow to qualify as F1 cars is complicated, but basically it covers two areas: rules of the races and construction of the car. Construction includes the car's body, engine, brakes, and steering. These rules are designed to make the cars as equal as possible, putting the emphasis on driving skill.

The Red Bull Technology factory has been the home of Red Bull Racing since 2004.

Formula 1 races are held as team competitions, with each team having two cars per race. Examples of top teams today include Infiniti Red Bull Racing, Scuderia Ferrari, and Williams Martini Racing.

Formula 1 cars are open-wheel cars, meaning that their wheels are on the outside of the car, unlike a normal passenger car or stock car, where the wheels are placed inside the car's fenders.

Formula 1 cars are called "single-seaters" because they have only one seat in the front of the car where the driver sits.

The Constructor

Formula 1 teams must build, or construct, the chassis of their race cars. The chassis is basically the skeleton of the car. Because of this rule, F1 fans often refer to both "team" and "**constructor**" to mean the same thing. The team that scores the most points with its chassis wins the World Constructors' Championship.

Each Formula 1 race has points to be won by the top drivers and constructors. At the end of the season, the points for all the drivers and constructors are added up, and those with the highest totals are declared champions.

Each race has points awarded as follows:

1st: 25 points	**6th**: 8 points
2nd: 18 points	**7th**: 6 points
3rd: 15 points	**8th**: 4 points
4th: 12 points	**9th**: 2 points
5th: 10 points	**10th**: 1 point

The final race of the season is worth double the point totals above.

Sebastian Vettel celebrates winning a World Championship. He is among the most successful F1 drivers of all time.

The Car

The vehicles you see every day on streets and highways, and those racing in Formula 1, can both be called "cars," but that is where the similarity ends! In fact, a Formula 1 car has more in common with a fighter plane than it does with a regular car. That's because the shape of F1 cars is key to making the cars go as fast as they do. They are designed with aerodynamics in mind, meaning they have shapes that let them slice through the air as easily as possible, making them faster. Formula 1 cars can easily attain speeds of 200 mph (322 km/h). During a race, when making turns or battling with other cars, the speeds are generally lower.

Engines like this Lotus Renault Formula 1 can be seen at race car trade shows.

The FIA controls every design detail of modern F1 race cars such as this one.

The Engine

As of 2014 the F1 car has a 1.6-liter V6 turbo engine. This new engine is more energy efficient, but still very powerful. F1 engines generate power by running at a rotational speed of up to 15,000 revolutions per minute (RPM). A road car of about the same size runs at about 6,000 RPM.

The steering wheel has all the controls for the car.

The Tires

Formula 1 tires are made of nylon and other materials that are much lighter than the rubber used for regular car tires. These special racing tires are strong in construction, but don't last very long. They need to be changed about every 75 miles (121 kilometers).

The Driver

Formula 1 rules make sure the cars that line up at the start of each race are very similar. That means that, often, the skill of the individual driver is what decides a race's winner. To be a top driver, you need to be mentally sharp and physically fit. F1 racing is very demanding, and it takes thousands of hours of practice to become good at it.

The whole Formula 1 team celebrates when their driver wins a race.

Drivers use all kinds of strategies and tactics to try to win races. Although it might seem logical to think that all race planning is about speed, actually the opposite is true. A key part of racing is stopping! Drivers must take into account how often they will need to stop for things like tire changes. Given the high speeds of F1 cars, they burn through tires very quickly, so, in addition to realizing what is happening on the track, drivers need to know when they must take breaks. Nothing slows you down more than blowing a tire!

Formula 1 drivers need to think of many things in order to win a race.

Staying Protected

High-tech equipment is crucial for drivers to stay safe in a race. They wear a full protective suit, as well as boots, gloves, and a helmet. The protective suit, or overalls, is made from a synthetic fiber called Nomex. Although no driver wants or plans to get in a crash, this material will protect a driver from a fire for at least 12 seconds. Within that time, rescue crews are usually able to reach an accident and assist the driver.

Drivers have to adjust their tactics when racing in rain.

Racing Circuits

Formula 1 races are held on different kinds of courses. Each has its own challenges, and all of them make for exciting competition as the drivers adapt to the different conditions.

There are three basic types of Formula 1 courses, or **circuits**:

- racetrack
- city street track
- hybrid track

Britain's Silverstone racetrack, an airfield during World War II, hosts the British Grand Prix.

A racetrack is one that has been specifically built for auto racing with several turns, curves, and straights. Many fans of Formula 1 racing consider this the "classic" or "proper" form of Formula 1.

The Circuit de Barcelona-Catalunya in Spain features long straights and a variety of corners.

A city street track is actually made up of city streets, specially adapted for racing. Monaco, Melbourne, and Singapore are examples of street circuits. Of course, regular traffic is prevented from using the roads on race day!

A hybrid track, such as Montreal, combines both the racetrack and city street in a single race.

F1 cars race on the city streets of Valencia Street Circuit in Spain during the Grand Prix of Europe.

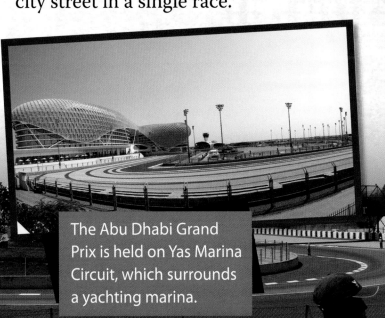

The Abu Dhabi Grand Prix is held on Yas Marina Circuit, which surrounds a yachting marina.

⚠ FAST FACT

An important part of any F1 course is the run-off zone. There are several of these areas, placed around the track, which are built to help slow down cars that have gone out of control, and prevent them from slamming into track walls or other cars.

Famous Circuits

Monaco Grand Prix is a tough, hilly course.

There are many famous Formula 1 racetracks around the world. Some have been around since the early days of Formula 1, while others are relatively new.

Monaco Grand Prix is a street circuit in the Principality of Monaco, near France. Racing fans sometimes also call this Grand Prix the "Monte Carlo." A championship has been held there since before the actual start of Formula 1 racing, with the first race happening in 1929. Many drivers consider Monaco to be one of the toughest courses in all of Formula 1 because of its many hills and tight corners. For example, Monaco has one of the slowest corners, which drivers pass through at about 30 mph (48 km/h), and one of the fastest straightaways, which they drive at over 160 mph (257 km/h)!

Circuit of the Americas is in Texas.

Hockenheimring alternates as the site of the German Grand Prix, and, unlike Monaco, is very flat. It is also well-known for hosting drag races, and musical events and concerts. There are seats for 120,000 people to watch racing there. The current course is just over 4 miles (6.4 km) long. The Finnish driver Kimi Raikkonen has recorded the fastest lap ever on it, at 1 minute, 13.780 seconds.

Hockenheimring (above) and Nürburgring GP–Strecke alternate yearly as hosts of the German Grand Prix.

Circuit of the Americas in Austin, Texas, has been the home of the United States Grand Prix since 2012. It is just over 5.5 miles (8.9 km) long and hosts all kinds of auto and motorcycle races. It is the first course in the United States to be built especially for Formula 1 racing, and can hold over 110,000 fans on race day.

Race Day

A lot goes on at a Formula 1 race, which in fact takes up an entire weekend. On Fridays, the drivers take their practice runs, getting used to how their cars perform on the track and in the specific weather conditions.

Saturday is qualifying day, as drivers compete against the clock. The driver with the fastest time in qualifying wins the prestigious pole position on race day, which takes place on Sunday.

At the races fans get chances to see cars up close and meet the drivers.

Formula 1 driver Jenson Button does some burnouts for his fans during race weekend.

Lining Up

On race day, the cars hit the track for warm-up laps 30 minutes before the actual start. At the start, cars line up in the order of their qualifying times. A green light tells drivers when they can start the slow formation lap. On this lap, the drivers make sure everything is in order with their cars. The cars then return to their assigned spot on the starting grid, and the race begins!

PODIUM FINISH

At the end of each race, the top three drivers climb a podium, where they stand as the national anthem of the race winner's home country is played. Famous people from the host country present trophies to the drivers. The winning team gets the constructor's trophy. Then the real fun begins, as the winning drivers spray each other and the fans with champagne!

Sebastian Vettel of Red Bull Racing Team receives the trophy from Malaysia's Prime Minister at the podium in Sepang, Malaysia.

The Race

Twenty-two cars (11 teams of two drivers each) currently compete in each Formula 1 race. Speed is essential if any driver wants to win, but of course, each Grand Prix race involves a lot more than simply driving as fast as you can.

Drivers also need to follow the race rules, or risk heavy penalties and even disqualification. During a race, officials display certain colors of **flags** to let the drivers know what is going on, and what they can and cannot do on the track.

A track marshal waves the yellow warning flag after a track incident.

Formula 1 drivers line up their race cars to their allocated spots before the start of a race.

⚠ FAST FACT

Drivers don't have to rely only on the flag system for warnings. A display in each driver's cockpit, called the GPS marshaling system, lights up with the flag color when the driver passes the affected section of track.

Formula 1 Racing Flags

Green Flag
This is the all-clear flag. It tells drivers they have passed a danger spot on the track, and the yellow flag danger period is over.

Red Flag
This flag means the race has been stopped. The cause is usually unsafe conditions brought on by bad weather or a bad accident.

Yellow Flag
There is a potentially hazardous situation; drivers slow down and keep their position.

Black Flag
This tells a driver to return to the pit. It is usually waved with a car number, and often indicates that a driver is being disqualified.

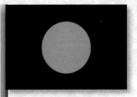

Black Flag with Orange Disk
Driver is to leave the track because of a mechanical problem. It is waved with a car number.

Yellow Flag with Red Stripes
This flag warns drivers when there is debris, fluid, or oil on the track.

Light Blue Flag
The driver is about to be overtaken by faster drivers and must yield to them.

White Flag
This flag warns drivers to slow down because there is a slow-moving vehicle, such as an ambulance, ahead.

Checkered Flag
Race is over. All drivers want to see the checkered flag waved at them first, as that means they have won!

Pit Stop Action

It is important to remember that even though each car has only one driver, there are many members on a Formula 1 team who contribute to the car's performance.

The **pit crew** works on the car when it comes into the **pit** for tire changes and repairs. It is essential that these pit stops be done as effectively and quickly as possible, because every second spent in the pits is lost time on the track. On the other hand, doing a poor job in the pits will slow a car down and perhaps even cause an accident. In Formula 1, the typical pit stop lasts less than three seconds!

Pit crew members must practice the procedure many, many times to be able to do their job in three seconds.

Meet the Pit Crew

There are between 14 to 20 people in each pit crew. Each crew member has a specific job. Some are responsible for jacking the car up so that the tires can be changed. Some members of the crew remove old wheels, while others put on new ones. Pit crews practice many times so that the pit stop service is fast and safe. The pit crew members often wear protective clothing and helmets while in the **pit lane**.

NO GAS!

Unlike other types of car racing, F1 pit crews are not allowed to add or remove fuel from a car during the race. This rule came into effect in 2010.

The cars must start the race with enough fuel to last the entire race. This makes pit stops safer. With no fueling to do, the pit crew now concentrates on changing tires. F1 drivers usually schedule one, two, or three pit stops as part of their racing strategy.

Formula 1 pit stops revolve around replacing the tires.

Crash Course

The FIA, racing teams, and race organizers all work together to make sure drivers, pit crews, and fans stay safe during a race. This involves making sure cars are built and maintained as well as possible, keeping drivers safe with the right equipment, and keeping the tracks safe.

Formula 1 drivers wear a full protective suit that will shield them from a fire until the rescue crews arrive. Also, drivers wear a piece of protective equipment called the Head and Neck Support (**HANS**) system, which sits on the neck and shoulders and works, along with the driver's helmet, for protection.

Formula 1 drivers are strapped into their car's cockpit by a six-point harness, just like the ones found in fighter jets.

The HANS device is a safety item required in many car racing sports.

Driving in a Cocoon

Formula 1 cars are built with what is called a "**survival cell.**" The cell is similar in shape to a bathtub. It's an extremely strong section of the car built not to fall apart if an accident happens. To accomplish this, the single seat is designed to fit a driver's exact size. The seat must be low enough to keep the driver's head from sticking out too much. Otherwise the driver could be gravely injured in a crash.

THE SAFETY CAR

One car that does not actually take part in the race is vital for driver, pit crew, and fan safety. This is the **safety car**. If there is a dangerous situation, such as wet conditions, this car takes to the track and drives to the front of the field, leading the cars around the track at lower speeds until the danger has passed. When the safety car is on the track, no passing is allowed.

At the end of the caution period, the safety car leaves the track and the competitors may resume racing.

Formula 1 Stars

It takes a lot of hard work to become an F1 star. These drivers need great fitness to keep up with the demands of racing, and also need solid educations to be able to understand complicated race plans and how their cars operate.

Fernando Alonso competes for Scuderia Ferrari.

FERNANDO ALONSO

This Spanish driver won World Championships in 2005 and 2006. He had a very successful career as a kart driver, winning a world championship in that form of racing in 1996. He drove in his first F1 race in 2001.

SEBASTIAN VETTEL

German driver Sebastian Vettel is considered one of the best drivers of all time, with four World Championships in a row, from 2010 to 2013. In 2010, at age 23, he was the youngest winner in history. As you might expect from someone who has had so much success so young, he started driving karts at the age of three!

Sebastian Vettel drives for Red Bull Racing.

LEWIS HAMILTON

Born in 1985, British driver Lewis Hamilton won the Formula 1 World Championship in 2008. Legend has it that as a 10-year-old, he walked up to the head of the McLaren team and told him he would one day race for them! Hamilton worked his way up the racing ranks to drive in his first F1 race in 2007. As the first black F1 driver, he has faced unfortunate racism from fans at times.

AYRTON SENNA: THE ALL-TIME GREATEST

Many fans consider the Brazilian driver Ayrton Senna to be the best driver to ever take part in Formula 1 racing. Born in 1960, he won three World Championships in 1988, 1990, and 1991. Sadly, he was killed in a Grand Prix race while leading in Italy in 1994. Senna was the last driver to die in a Formula 1 race as his accident caused many safety measures to be put in place.

Lewis Hamilton races for Mercedes AMG.

Ayrton Senna had 41 Grand Prix Wins, 80 podium finishes and 610 career points.

You and Formula 1

Even though you might not be a champion F1 driver yet, there is a lot you can do to get involved in this kind of racing.

Watching your favorite driver in action is always a great thrill.

Formula 1 races are shown widely on TV, and there are lots of videos and information on the Internet. If you are lucky, there may even be a Grand Prix or other open-wheel race near your home. It is also easy to follow the results of your favorite driver or team as they race for the Championships. That is a great way to build an interest in the sport.

When you attend a race with your family, there is always a good chance to meet your favorite driver and get an autograph.

Driver's Education

Remember that getting a good education in school is also important for a Formula 1 driver. Learning to drive a high-tech car, understanding complicated race instructions, working as part of a team, and being able to talk to the media are skills you begin to learn in school.

A good way of getting introduced to car racing is to attend a race school.

With an adult's permission you can also try racing yourself. Start with go-karts or Quarter Midget cars.

Glossary

circuit The track, or course, on which an F1 race is held.

constructor The builder of an F1 race car; also known as the race "team."

FIA Fédération Internationale de l'Automobile is the French name for the organization that controls auto racing.

flag The banner that race officials use to send signals to drivers during an F1 race.

Formula 1 A form of auto racing featuring open-wheel cars that follow a set "formula" for their construction. Also known as F1.

Grand Prix A French term meaning "big prize" that is used as the name of any big F1 event.

HANS The Head and Neck Support (HANS) system, equipment used by F1 drivers to prevent injuries to these crucial areas.

pit The area of the track where teams can change tires and perform repairs to a car in mid-race.

pit crew The team of people that services a race car.

pit lane The road from the pits to the track where cars are started and serviced.

safety car The car used by race officials to drive at the front of the pack to slow the other cars down during times when it is unsafe to race.

survival cell The part of an F1 car that is built with very strong materials designed to keep a driver safe in the event of a crash.

For More Information

Further Reading

Buckley Jr., James. *The Official BBC Sport Guide: Formula One 2014.* Carlton, 2014.

Georgiou, Tyrone. *Formula 1.* Gareth Stevens Publishing, 2011.

Hamilton, John. *Formula One Cars.* ABDO Publishing Company, 2012.

Websites

Due to the changing nature of Internet links, PowerKids Press has developed an online list of websites related to the subject of this book. This site is updated regularly. Please use this link to access the list: **www.powerkidslinks.com/tcf/for1**

Index